Slightly Off Center!

Slightly *off* Center!

Growth Principles to Thaw Frozen Paradigms

TERRY CAMSEY

Crest Books
Salvation Army National Publications
Alexandria, Virginia

Published by Crest Books, Salvation Army National Publications
615 Slaters Lane, Alexandria, Virginia 22313
(703) 684-5500 Fax: (703) 684-5539
http://publications.salvationarmyusa.org

Printed in the United States of America

Layout and design by Kristin B. Griffin
Cover design by Kristin B. Griffin

Library of Congress Catalog Card Number: 00–101144

ISBN: 0–9657601–8–9

To my friend and mentor,
Carl F. George,
who first ignited the passion.

Contents

Foreword

Major Terry Camsey has never been satisfied with things as they are. For a decade he has immersed himself in the disturbing literature of church growth theory. He has applied his alert, creative and restless mind to the search for answers as to how churches grow and how the full potential for Salvation Army corps to grow healthfully and vigorously can best be realized. He has traveled across the world in his quest and has been a major player in releasing the growth potential of corps while conducting countless assessments, seminars and workshops across North America, Australia and the United Kingdom.

In this series of cleverly conceived and pithily powerful essays, Camsey sets a burr under the saddle of complacency and stirs us to thought and action. And that is what is needed most—a willingness to risk and pay the price of honesty and action. Camsey writes with buoyant optimism concerning the growth potential of Army corps. But he has long since abandoned the luxury of viewing corps life through rose–tinted lenses. With penetrating insight, he identifies the perspectives and paradigms that tend to distort our vision. Impatient to help us see things as they are, he sharpens our focus while challenging our assumptions. His gift for creative use of memorable metaphors and striking analogies captures our imagination and makes the correction of our comfortable misconceptions more tolerable.

There is a great deal of solid, if sometimes painful, truth in these pages. They merit careful reflection and open discussion. But they will have missed their mark if they do not lead to corrective strategies and bold, prayerful action.

General Paul A. Rader (R)

Preface

For many denominations crunch time has arrived. After decades of plateau, followed by steady decline in memberships and attendance, the end is finally in sight.

Trends on graphs can be projected to the point where they intersect the horizontal axis of history—a moment in time when without intervention the denomination can write its own epitaph.

It doesn't have to be so! An honest appraisal and acceptance of reality can free denominations to recognize that "more of the same" simply is not a viable option.

Reassessment of methods and—more importantly—of the principles that such methods were designed to implement can be the catalyst that releases creative re–engineering of more effective strategies for the future.

Unfortunately, over the years, a gradual decay of passion for the lost may have led to ministry myopia, where those in a position to take corrective action have "frozen paradigms," fixed views of what they perceive to be reality which may not be complete and may, in fact, be dead wrong!

This book aims to thaw such frozen paradigms by throwing them slightly off center. It is designed for all who have an interest in and a responsibility for the extension of the kingdom of God. This publication is for reading, teaching and for stimulating discussion in group settings.

What does the Spirit say to the churches?

Notes on Discussion Questions

If you were asked to prescribe for a dozen people a regimen of diet and exercise to get them into peak condition, the prescription for each would differ. That is because it would depend on their present state of health. The situation is no different for corps or other churches; their effectiveness depends very much on their responses to local institutional and contextual conditions.

To enable each corps to derive the maximum benefit from this book, I include discussion questions for each topic. These follow a simple format.

First, at the end of each topic additional thoughts are included to ponder. These help to sharpen our focus on the subject under review.

Then I list three simple questions to help you probe the situation in your corps. They are based on questions used frequently by Lyle E. Schaller, dean of North American Church Growth Consultants. These questions start to explore the impact of the subject in the local context.

Third, I suggest that time be spent considering how to make the situation better. The goal is to brainstorm a minimum of ten things you might do. Invariably, your better ideas will emerge around number five or six! From these, select two or three as the first course of action.

Finally, I include scriptural affirmations which collectively assure us that in the end we (Christ's Body) win!

Joshua told the people, "consecrate yourselves, for tomorrow the Lord will do amazing things among you." (Joshua 3:5)

Part One

Exploring Growth Inhibitors

This section contains two diagnostic questions to help you determine the most pressing issues in your corps, plus twelve provocative, paradigm–enlarging concepts to explore.

Two Questions

Imagine it is 10 years from now. The unthinkable has happened: the corps has died. Why?

If you could wave a magic wand today and immediately solve one problem that could keep your corps from dying, what would it be?

These two questions penetrate to the heart of present concerns and, if asked corporately, they can help a corps council develop an agenda for growth. It is suggested that each participant be given two index cards, each of a different color so that answers to the questions are not confused. Participants are advised not to write their names on the cards. This tactic will free people to write down what they feel, rather than what they think the consultant wants to hear.

Ask the participants to use one color card to respond to the first question after you have read it. Collect the cards and shuffle them. Repeat the exercise for question two.

Sort each pile. You will see that the answers, by and large, will fall into these categories: program, purse, premises, property/possessions, procedures/processes. Or, perhaps the answers might fall under the five roles set out in "How Is Your Balance?" (pg. 16): nurture, evangelism, worship, ministry to the body, ministry to the community. You may also be able to determine from the number of similar responses which matters are the most pressing to the majority of people.

Follow up by pointing out that since the questions referred to what participants visualize happening ten years from now, there is time to prevent the problems from becoming terminal.

Ponder

The above questions are powerful diagnostic tools. Because

input comes from anonymous participants, it will often bring issues to the surface and stimulate dialogue on common concerns.

The second question is particularly powerful because it identifies which issues are of primary importance to the individual. It is amazing how in an atmosphere of anonymity common concerns surface.

The findings from both questions can form the basis of an ongoing agenda as you strive to remove the stumbling blocks and take proactive steps to move on.

Probe

1. What symptoms of this situation do we see in our corps?
2. Why are things that way?
3. Is this good or bad?

Pursue

How can we improve the situation? Look for 10 ways and pick the best.

Jesus looked at them and said, "With man this is impossible, but with God all things are possible." (Matthew 19:26)

The Old Tap Insanity Test

The story is told of a test used at one time in the United States to determine whether someone was insane. The subject was taken to a sink into which water was gushing from a tap. The person was given a cup and asked to empty the sink. Those who turned off the tap were judged to be sane!

If in trying to improve the health and effectiveness of a corps we try to fix the symptoms instead of the root cause, we are like the subject who desperately tries to empty the sink with the cup.

Will fixing the old model do, or will that only restore a model that, though in working condition, may be outdated? Is a return to the "stagnant quo" helpful?

I was once told the story of a young man who inherited the family drill–making business. At the first board meeting he attended he said, "Gentlemen, we are not in the business of making drills ... we are in the business of making holes!"

A very astute observation, since we now know that lasers make better holes and, who knows, maybe one day someone will ask, "Why do we make holes? Isn't there a better way to do this?"

What are the symptoms causing our distress? What are the root causes? What is the cup and what is the tap? Be sure to diagnose problems accurately before prescribing what may cure nothing and only serve to alleviate symptoms.

Ponder

It can be frustrating to think that you have found a solution to a problem, only to find that the solution makes no lasting improvement at all. Often this is because the problem identified is only a symptom of the underlying cause.

How would you feel if you went to a doctor with pain and,

without any diagnosis, he prescribed aspirin? What if you later found out you had cancer?

The best way I have found to get at the underlying cause of a problem is to take the problem as presented and to ask, "Why is this a problem?" Then list all the reasons you can think of and ask of each, "Why is this a problem?" Take this process back through five "Whys?" and the causes will emerge. It is solutions to the causes that we seek. (See "Peel Off the Onion Skin," pg. 76)

Try this process of diagnosis to get at the real causes.

Probe

1. What symptoms of this situation do we see in our corps?
2. Why are things that way?
3. Is this good or bad?

Pursue

How can we improve the situation? Look for 10 ways and pick the best.

So then, each of us will give an account of himself to God. (Romans 14:12)

Why Young Adults Leave

Looking at the membership statistics of many corps, it is apparent that there are lots of junior soldiers, lots of over–fifty–five–year–olds and a dearth of adults between the ages of 20 to 55. The missing generations are, of course, the Baby Boomers (born 1946–1964) and the Baby Busters (born 1965–1983 or so).

Heavy losses take place at age 14, when many junior soldiers elect not to become senior soldiers. The drop is less drastic in corps with strong music sections (probably because it is the "family thing" to join those sections), but nevertheless it occurs.

In some territories, anywhere between 92% and 97% of youth recruits do not transfer to senior soldiership. That is a tremendous loss. There is a hole in the YP bucket!

At the same time, there is a tremendous amount of work going on among young people. If one asks, "Why?" the response is likely to be, "They are the Army of the future." In reality, they are the transient Army of today. Young people are introduced to the Army through youth programs at an early age but leave before they reach their teens. The average age of the water in the leaky bucket of YP work rarely exceeds seven to 14 years old.

The challenge is two–fold: To plug the hole in the bucket and to reach the missing generations. If we do neither, then the future for many corps 20 years from now is rather bleak.

Why do they leave? Eddie Gibbs reports in "Winning Them Back," a study in Australia, England, Scotland and the USA of young adults ages 20–26, that among the prime reasons young people leave are: irrelevant programs (76%), boring worship (67%–97% in UK), doubts about religion (67%), their age (61%), church too demanding (48%), too many commitments required (47%–80% in UK).

Ponder

Do you see this happening in your corps? How many young people have either left the corps or taken a back seat?

I have yet to see a corps where substantial numbers of junior soldiers join the adult ranks at age 14. It's common for adults to say, "It's time for you to grow up and be like me!" While the young people say, "I'm not sure I want to be like you at this time (if ever!)" The situation is compounded if parents do not attend church. "Growing up" in that case means leaving church to be like Mom and Dad.

Yet the reality is that in many communities there are churches with a thriving youth ministry. Why? Because these churches demonstrate unconditional love. These are the churches that retain young people when they finally do mature (whether that's at age 16, 24 or 35!).

Probe

1. What symptoms of this situation do we see in our corps?
2. Why are things that way?
3. Is this good or bad?

Pursue

How can we improve the situation? Look for 10 ways and pick the best.

Where there is no revelation, the people cast off restraint ... (Proverbs 29:18)

When Push Comes to Shove

Compel! How do you feel when you read that word—resistant? Nobody likes being told what to do by someone else. That's why guilt is such a poor motivator.

Many years ago I was much more active as a musician in the Army. I was a bandsman in the International Staff Band, a bandsman and songster in a very busy corps in the United Kingdom and involved in at least six rehearsals a week. That is not counting extra rehearsals called when a section was going away for a weekend of ministry. No wonder that during a family dinner my three-year-old daughter commented, "That's my Dad. He lives in the band!"

Add to the schedule I've described the time that I "specialled" as a guest soloist at least once a month and you can see why I was resistant to extra, last-minute rehearsal demands by section leaders, especially when told it was my duty to be there, or that if I were not present I'd let the section down.

Compulsion through provocation of guilt or accusation of disloyalty is a poor motivator, yet was frequently used in days when leaders were demagogues (or, frequently, demi-gods!).

It's easy to interpret going out into the highways and byways, forcing people to come in, as "compelling." But another way to encourage church growth is to create such compelling events that people can't stay away for fear of missing something. That's an "attraction" strategy as opposed to taking the gospel to the people—the "proclamation" style which we were so good at in the early days of the Army.

Getting people to come once is one thing. Getting them to keep coming is another. Whatever the strategy, loving churches grow and growing churches love others!

Shouldn't we be compelled by such love? Are we?

Ponder

Do you want your corps' pews filled with people who are there because of duty or because they want to avoid feelings of guilt? Or would you prefer to see the corps packed with people who simply can't stay away for fear of missing something worthwhile?

The reality is that people will do what they want to do. And they want to do something when the benefits exceed the cost. Part of that cost may be that they do not feel welcome when they come and, if that is the case, the backdoor is likely to be open wide. There is little point in inviting people who, if they visit, are likely to be lost through the backdoor.

Visitors are the hottest prospects for membership. By coming, they indicate they are looking for a church. Do you know how many visitors you have? Do you know their names and addresses? Do you follow up on each in a timely and appropriate manner?

Probe

1. What symptoms of this situation do we see in our corps?
2. Why are things that way?
3. Is this good or bad?

Pursue

How can we improve the situation? Look for 10 ways and pick the best.

When He had finished speaking, He said to Simon, "Put out into deep water, and let down the nets for a catch." (Luke 5:4)

Are You Spinning Your Wheels?

Imagine that the wheel of a bicycle represents all the activities a corps is involved in. Imagine that the hub represents the purpose, vision and values of the corps—the "why" of its existence. The tire is in contact with the road, so we might consider the tire to be all the contacts the corps has with the public. Then consider each of the spokes as a program or activity undertaken by the corps.

It becomes immediately apparent that if the spokes are disconnected from either the hub or the rim holding the tire in place, the wheel will collapse. If even a few of the spokes are disconnected at one end or the other, the wheel will be weakened and will probably buckle.

It certainly would benefit any corps to examine its programs and activities to ensure that each is firmly connected to the hub (i.e. is helping the corps fulfill its purpose or reason for being) and to the rim holding the tire. If the latter is not true, it is likely that the corps programs and activities exist to serve the congregation rather than the lost.

Maybe some of the spokes will be found to be superfluous. Perhaps a corps would be better off concentrating on a few, strategically placed spokes with the others supporting those.

Again, the issue of balance (see "How Is Your Balance" pg. 16) raises its head. Perhaps those major spokes should be: nurture, evangelism, worship, ministry to the Body, ministry to the community. If each spoke were at the right tension relative to the others, the result would be a smooth, balanced ride.

Ponder

The first question to ask is whether your corps has a clear purpose or mission statement. If you haven't clarified what you are supposed to be doing, it will be difficult to determine whether or not what you do is helpful in accomplishing that purpose.

Second, ask yourself which activities actually play a part in drawing new people into the corps family. Ask of every activity, "How many people are now a part of the regular worshiping congregation as a result of the activities of this group?" You'll soon find out where time could be spent more wisely.

A follow up question might be, "Can this activity become more effective in attracting people who will become worshiping members of the congregation?" If not, you need to seriously consider a more effective use of the energy being put into that program.

Probe

1. What symptoms of this situation do we see in our corps?
2. Why are things that way?
3. Is this good or bad?

Pursue

How can we improve the situation? Look for 10 ways and pick the best.

Therefore I do not run like a man running aimlessly; I do not fight like a man beating the air. (1 Corinthians 9:26)

What Year Is It in Your Corps?

Whenever my wife and I visit a corps, I whisper to her, "What year is it in here?" We look at the way people are dressed, listen to the language used, check out the decorations, try to place the generation in which the music being used was popular, etc. We have found that in some parts of the world even the dress of Salvationists on the platform represents a generation preceding that of those in the congregation. This is a simple, provable fact in that tunics with lay–down collars are more recent than those with stand–up collars, and hats for women soldiers are more recent than bonnets.

I then ask my wife, "What year is it outside this corps?" If the world outside is in the twenty–first century and the year inside the hall is 1972, or 1950, or even 1890, then the corps will probably have a difficult time bridging the gap to younger generations—apart, of course, from those sons and daughters of the regiment who understand and enjoy the atmosphere of nostalgia that can permeate a corps.

This issue raises a serious question (especially in light of the challenge to reach young adults). If we are not retaining our young people, and not attracting young adults, where will the corps be when the present congregation is 20 years older?

Recently, during a Sunday night salvation meeting, a new song from an Army musical was sung congregationally with great gusto. From my position on the platform I could see the street through the glass door and wondered if someone wandered in what era they would place us in. The song was in the style of the 1890s!

Ponder

Think very carefully before you answer this question! Believe it or not, there are still corps where even the "new wine" of Bible translations more recent than the King James version is not accepted by the "old wineskin." And, when one considers the language used, the dress, the music, the decoration, the pictures, the posters displayed ... well, it can be like an exercise in time travel—backwards.

There is much to be said for nostalgia, and I am quite sure that a corps setting out to be deliberately nostalgic could garner a large crowd of disillusioned Salvationists who left because of change.

But the future does not lie with the nostalgic (even though they deserve all the love and care we can give them—they earned it as our forbears). The future lies with emerging generations. Booth saw that in his design of The Salvation Army. Do we?

Probe

1. What symptoms of this situation do we see in our corps?
2. Why are things that way?
3. Is this good or bad?

Pursue

How can we improve the situation? Look for 10 ways and pick the best.

A time to kill and a time to heal, a time to tear down and a time to build. (Ecclesiastes 3:3)

Which Package Would You Choose?

Imagine two boxes. They are both the same size. One box is wrapped up with newspaper and chewed–up string, the other with pretty silver foil and a bright, fluffy bow.

I go out on the street with a box in each hand and offer the first person I meet his choice of boxes. Which do you think he will choose?

Unless he is a very devious thinker, he will, in all probability, choose the prettier package, assuming that it must contain something more valuable than the one wrapped in newspaper. But what if each box actually contained exactly the same thing: a copy of the gospel message?

If we only offer the gospel in a box wrapped up in newspaper and chewed–up string, few people are going to be interested in exploring the contents. Packaging is important. Covers *do* sell books.

Sometimes corps do not thrive because the wrapper within which they enclose the gospel message is not attractive enough to encourage unbelievers to look more closely at what it has to offer.

The wrapping may include things like dress codes, times of meetings and style of worship. What is preventing people from opening your package? Should the salvation meeting be wrapped in a more attractive (to the unsaved) package than the holiness meeting?

Ponder

I once arrived late at a corps I was visiting. As I peeked through the double doors on the ground level, I saw a packed sanctuary with plush red carpeting, padded seats and a crowded platform.

There was no room downstairs, so I went up to the balcony. At the top of the stairs, the carpet disappeared to reveal bare wooden floorboards. The seats were old benches. Up in the balcony I found a few other congregants sitting in the midst of a big pile of junk, which could clearly be seen by those on the platform. Out of sight (of the downstairs congregation), out of mind. Had I not been a Salvationist, but a stranger to the Army, I would have had a problem sorting out the rationale. I should state, incidentally, that because I was late there was no one to greet me either.

I have been to many corps where there are similar accumulations of junk, poor decorations and dirty toilets. They are so familiar to the regular congregation that no one notices—except visitors, that is!

Probe

1. What symptoms of this situation do we see in our corps?
2. Why are things that way?
3. Is this good or bad?

Pursue

How can we improve the situation? Look for 10 ways and pick the best.

See, the former things have taken place, and new things I declare; before they spring into being I announce them to you. (Isaiah 42:9)

How Is Your Balance?

Can you imagine what would happen if only parts of a baby developed? If some parts grew normally but others just failed to mature, that baby would at best be malformed. At worst, it would not survive. In fact, if any of the human body systems (circulatory, nervous, digestive, skeletal, arterial, etc.) is out of kilter, the rest of the body is negatively affected.

The concept is no different for churches, the Body of Christ. It is, however, even more critical, since the church is to represent and act as Christ in its community. Not only should that body function well, but it needs to represent Christ to the community. It needs to be a healthy, virile, evangelically effective Christ. To do that, its systems need also to be well balanced.

Any study of what the Bible says about the purposes of church will, invariably, isolate five key functions: nurture (discipling the members of the body), evangelism (sharing the good news with the lost), worship (God–honoring, Christ–centered, Holy Spirit–empowered), ministry to the Body (encouragement and care of the members) and ministry to the community (meeting the needs of the community).

Naturally, the talk these days is of church health, not church growth, since healthy bodies grow!

So how is the balance in your corps? How do you allocate your purse, premises, possessions and people? Are you out of balance, and if so, what can be done to regain your equilibrium?

Ponder

Here's a challenge. Make a column on the left side of a page and list *nurture* (discipling, teaching: Bible study, witnessing, practice of agape love, prayer, personal ministry, giving, etc.), *evangelism* (outreach: open air meetings, activities to attract the unchurched, advertising, etc.), *worship* (encountering God), *service to the Body* (caring for attendees, encouraging, pastoring, building relationships, resolving crises), *service to the community* (bridge building through meeting unmet needs of people in the community). To the right rate how your corps performs each of these using a scale from 1–10 with 1 being "very poor" and 10 being "very good."

Add the ratings for each and divide by the number of people participating to calculate the group response. Compare the totals for each. The ratings will be a starting point for discussion.

Probe

1. What symptoms of this situation do we see in our corps?
2. Why are things that way?
3. Is this good or bad?

Pursue

How can we improve the situation? Look for 10 ways and pick the best.

If the Lord is pleased with us, He will lead us into that land, a land flowing with milk and honey, and will give it to us. (Numbers 14:8)

Where Are You on the Life Cycle?

To everything there is a season, according to the book of Ecclesiastes. A time to be born and a time to die, to plant and to uproot, to tear down and to build, to keep and to throw away.

Many things in this world have a cyclical life: products on shelves, businesses, humans, animals, weather, organizations, denominations, individual churches, small groups ...

Within the life cycle five key stages emerge:

Birth: Someone has a vision for what might be. They see it in their mind's eye and then set out to create it. People tend to be attracted to big, bold, beckoning visions, just as moths are attracted to a bright light.

Growth: Rapid expansion occurs as people strive to fulfill the vision.

Plateau: Eventually the growth levels off. Purpose is still remembered but passion starts to wane. If there is no positive intervention, the plateau will start to *decline* and doubts will set in. As purpose and vision fade, conflicts arise and nostalgia for the "good old days" abounds. The cycle is on its final arc toward *death.*

General Bramwell Tillsley (R), when elected General and earlier in the *Officer* magazine (1985), applied the life cycle paradigm to the Army, and expressed his fear that the movement (growth stage) was in danger of becoming an institution (i.e., plateau, or "museum," stage). When I ask a group of Salvationists to tell me where they think the Army is on its life cycle, they tell me it is between stages four and five, the decline and death phases. In other words, General Tillsley was optimistic!

What's the solution? Try a reaffirmation of purpose and a big, bold, beckoning vision!

Ponder

God definitely knew what He was doing when He limited the child–bearing years. Ecclesiastes 3:2 refers specifically to this: "There is a time to be born and a time to die." There is a window of opportunity in which to ensure the continuity of the family line by having children. These days all is not necessarily lost, even if one parent becomes infertile, since through the services of surrogate mothers having a child is not impossible. We must not forget, either, that with God's intervention even the aged Sarah gave birth, though she laughingly thought it was impossible.

It is the same for a church. The most natural and, in fact, easiest births are possible in the early years when a newly planted church has grown through its own childhood and adolescence and is still healthy enough to bear a child. Not that it is impossible later—we have a God who specializes in accomplishing the impossible. That new birth, with its assurance of vitality for another generation, starts as in human life with a vision that is turned into reality by the parents. Where are you on the life cycle? Is it time to envision another generation and make it a reality?

Probe

1. What symptoms of this situation do we see in our corps?
2. Why are things that way?
3. Is this good or bad?

Pursue

How can we improve the situation? Look for 10 ways and pick the best.

What has been will be again, what has been done will be done again; there is nothing new under the sun. (Ecclesiastes 1:9)

How Long Is Your Memory?

Did you ever hear the story of the little boy who set out for school one winter morning? He arrived late and the teacher questioned his tardiness.

"Well, sir," he said, "the pavements were so icy that, for every step forward I took, I slipped back two!"

"So," asked the teacher, "how did you get here?"

"Simple," said the boy, "I just walked home!"

Professor Robert Webber has suggested that the problem most denominations face is getting beyond the "immediate past" to the "past past." You can see what he means. In their early days, most denominations had a strong, mutually understood purpose and vision. They were passionate about ministry and prepared to take risks, even if that meant failure at times.

Its leaders were of a more entrepreneurial than managerial nature. They were much more concerned about doing the right things than about doing things right. There was an optimism in the air. They were confident that the world would be won in their lifetime, and they possessed an energy to match that hope.

But as purpose and vision fade, means can become confused with ends. Rules, regulations and policies can become more and more restrictive of initiative. It can be the kiss of death!

We need to recall and recapture the spirit of those early days ... and rediscover the joy of trying, failing, trying again and winning!

Ponder

When stationed in the United Kingdom I made a special effort to speak to retired officers as frequently as possible, primarily because they command such respect and can influence change for better or worse. At the beginning of my talk a number of these officers would be sitting with crossed arms (with a "bless me if you can" attitude) because they knew I would be addressing the need for change and adaptation.

However, as I talked of the life cycle and its characteristics at various lifestages, arms would unfold and smiles would appear. I was stirring distant memories of times when we were not always as stuffy as we have become. Memories were unearthed of times when we were flexible and fun–loving, times when it was sheer joy to be around the corps.

Someone said there are two reasons people don't become Christians. First, because they've never seen one, second, because they have!

"Am I what once I was? ... Have I the zeal I had?" (*The Salvation Army Song Book*, 409).

Probe

1. What symptoms of this situation do we see in our corps?
2. Why are things that way?
3. Is this good or bad?

Pursue

How can we improve the situation? Look for 10 ways and pick the best.

Forget the former things; do not dwell on the past. (Isaiah 43:18)

What Do You See?

Paradigms. A neat word that describes the way an individual views things. Show an optimist a glass with water up to its midpoint and she will tell you it is half–full. Show a pessimist the same glass and he will tell you it is half–empty. The reality, of course, is that it is both half–full and half–empty.

This metaphor can be applied to any growth challenge. You'll see the optimists at work hoping for the best, concentrating on potentials with little regard for obstacles. You'll also observe the pessimists who tend to disparage any efforts because they see none of the possibilities.

What we really need is for the optimists and pessimists to talk to each other. They first need to understand what the other sees. Then, in light of all the information that has surfaced, they must agree to work together to solve the challenges identified.

What do you see? Are you open to the views of others who may see things differently?

Ponder

I love the story of the two battleships on maneuvers in heavy weather. Visibility was poor due to fog, and the captain stayed on deck to keep an eye on things.

In the dark, one of the sailors called out a warning that there was a light on the starboard bow. The captain asked whether it was moving or steady, fearing a collision with another ship. The sailor told him it was steady, which indicated they were on a collision course with another ship. The captain told him to signal the other ship to change course. The response from the operator of the light indicated that the first ship should change course.

"Tell him I'm the captain, and that he should change course," said the captain. The reply came back: "I'm a seaman second–class, you'd better change course!"

The captain, angered at the junior officer's insolence told his man to signal "I'm a battleship ... you'd be advised to change course."

Back came the reply, "I am a lighthouse!"

Probe

1. What symptoms of this situation do we see in our corps?
2. Why are things that way?
3. Is this good or bad?

Pursue

How can we improve the situation? Look for 10 ways and pick the best.

See, the Lord your God has given you the land. Go up and take possession of it as the Lord, the God of your fathers told you. Do not be afraid; do not be discouraged. (Deuteronomy 1:21)

Even Inside the Box ...

Imagine that the Army is like a box. In fact, let's think of it as a larger box ... a big room ... a sanctuary. There are people outside of that sanctuary and there are others inside it.

Those inside do not necessarily see the same thing. For example, ask those sitting in the pews of the sanctuary to describe what they see and they'll describe the platform. Ask those on the platform to describe what they see and they'll describe the back of the sanctuary.

Ask the songsters sitting on one side of the sanctuary (at right angles to the platform) what they see and they'll describe the wall in front of them. Ask the singing company sitting opposite and they'll describe the other wall. If someone lay on their back and looked up, he'd describe the ceiling. If someone could be suspended from the ceiling looking down, she'd describe the floor.

Which these people is right? All of them! Each sees a part of the whole, but none of them is seeing the whole. It can be that way with various corps sections. Each section sees some of the picture, but not necessarily the whole. It can be that way in any corps. Some see feast and think that's the way it is everywhere. Some see famine and think the same.

Mrs. Commissioner Winifred Pender (R) spoke once of a view she enjoyed from a hill. On one occasion, a tree had developed thick foliage and obstructed the view. The view had not altered, but she had to change position to see it clearly. Perhaps changing your position might help in your present situation?

Ponder

The more we look at something, the less we see it! I remember when my kids were small, one of them used a crayon on the bathroom wall. I agreed with my wife that I would clean the wall "tomorrow." Tomorrow came and I was too busy. I forgot. The next day I didn't even notice the crayon marks.

It can be like that in the corps. We can be so familiar with the bit of activity we're involved in that we lose sight of the big picture altogether. We think that the totality of the Army is merely a multiplication of what we alone see.

It doesn't hurt, once in a while, to approach an issue from another point of view. It will challenge your tunnel vision while enlarging your understanding.

Is there a "whole" or a "hole" in your perception of what the Army is?

Probe

1. What symptoms of this situation do we see in our corps?
2. Why are things that way?
3. Is this good or bad?

Pursue

How can we improve the situation? Look for 10 ways and pick the best.

But blessed are your eyes, for they see; and your ears for they hear. (Matthew 13:16)

The Outsider's View Is Just As Valid!

What those outside the Army see is just as valid for them as our view is valid for us. However, they don't necessarily see things from our perspective, and often we are ignorant of theirs.

For example, we know that many recognize the uniform we wear, but not as many as we would hope. Many a time at the airport I have been asked questions about flights. When one lady asked what airline I represented, I said, "Heavenly United!" It's easy to assume that because they recognize the uniform, they know we are committed Christians, but that is not necessarily so. Some see us as a kind of Christian Red Cross.

I remember one Boomer in a focus group suddenly realizing that "Salvation" in our name means "converted." He thought that we came to the salvation of people in need, which we do, but that's only part of the message. Another thought that the "Fire" in "Blood and Fire" meant hell. Why wouldn't he?

If we want them to know we are Christians by our dress (the uniform has little to tell them we are Christian), we are going to have to either tell them or put some wording or recognizable logo on the uniform!

And, if they think that we are all "down and outers" who get our clothes from Salvation Army thrift stores, and that is not a message many may want to give, it will take conscious steps to change that perception in their minds.

Perception is not necessarily the position you hold, but it certainly is the position people think you hold!

Ponder

It happened again the other day. We live in San Pedro,

California, which is where the cruise ships depart. My wife in her fatigue uniform was shopping in the grocery store and someone asked her which boat she worked on. Of course you never can think quickly enough in such a situation, otherwise her answer would have been, "The Love Boat, of course!"

It pays to challenge assumptions. It also pays to get the full picture even if reality is not what we wish it were or think it should be. I have known of administrative areas of the Army that have spent a great deal of money to sponsor in–depth research only to sweep the results under the rug because the research findings were not what they wanted to hear.

That is the danger: ignoring the larger reality by looking only for input that bolsters our current comfortable perceptions. That road can lead to the death of a corps.

Probe

1. What symptoms of this situation do we see in our corps?
2. Why are things that way?
3. Is this good or bad?

Pursue

How can we improve the situation? Look for 10 ways and pick the best.

Then the nations around you that remain will know that I the Lord have rebuilt what was destroyed and have replanted what was desolate. I the Lord have spoken, and I will do it. (Ezekiel 36:36)

Part Two

Aging Brings Its Own Challenges

This section explores some of the aspects of traditionalism that have an impact on ministry. Organizations change over time. Aging brings tension between older and younger generations, and Satan is very active in trying to widen the gap.

Words to Ponder

What if we sacrifice the living for the dead? Divert attention from the present holy war? Why must more die while those who could help dwell in modern ghettos of a time now gone? Perhaps some evil force would have it so ... And they still die. Diversionary tactics? Is that why?

—adapted from Ruth Bell Graham

These haunting words challenge us to consider the possibility that we may be selfishly putting our personal comfort before the need to win souls.

Have we in some places become "modern ghettos of a time now gone"? Have we somehow become frozen in time? The Amish are a quaint part of our social landscape, but we don't see people flocking to join their lifestyle. Do we want to be quaint, or do we want to be evangelically effective in today's society? Are we becoming more of a cultural artifact than a world–changing force? Is the notion of a "Salvation Amish" too great a stretch of the imagination?

Nothing living stands still, so the notion of trying to freeze ourselves into a time capsule seems ridiculous. Yet, is it not the nature of organizations to gradually become more and more regimented and less and less flexible? Someone wrote that everything crystallized at Booth's death. Did it?

If you were to list every mainline corps program, then look into the history books to see when those programs were first introduced, you'd find that some have certainly changed names: Chums to Cubs, Life Saving Guards to Guards or Brownies. You will also find that most of these programs were actually in place within five years of William Booth's death. Sobering, isn't it?

There is nothing that the Evil One would like better than to see us revering artifacts that were once vibrant, if that helps to take our eyes off the needs of the younger generations around us. People's needs today bear little resemblance to those for which Booth originally developed his programs. "Diversionary tactics"—there's a great deal of potential truth in that phrase.

Ponder

The thought that we might be "ghettos of a time now gone," diverting attention from our primary task and leaving people to die in sin is frightening.

Thank God there are signs that the Spirit is enlivening us again, and challenging us to rethink our priorities in light of the purpose for which we exist. God's purpose in sending His Son was so "that they may have life, and have it to the full" (John 10:10) This is a purpose which we, as the Body of Christ, must also adopt.

Anything that hinders the growth of the kingdom is not of God. If it is not of God, there is only one other possible source: Satan. God can make our blind eyes see, if that's what we really want.

Probe

1. What symptoms of this situation do we see in our corps?
2. Why are things that way?
3. Is this good or bad?

Pursue

How can we improve the situation? Look for 10 ways and pick the best.

See, I am doing a new thing! Now it springs up; do you not perceive it? I am making a way in the desert and streams in the wasteland. (Isaiah 43:19)

The Greatest Threat to Survival

The greatest threat to corps survival is undoubtedly the polarization of the young and old generations. Here we need to make a point. You cannot tell a person's age by the wrinkles on their face! There are old people who think young, and there are young people who think old—the latter often being sons and daughters of the regiment who have been exposed to Army culture over many years and through generations of forbears. Growing up having "roast officer" for Sunday lunch over many years can color perceptions of the Army.

The real difficulty comes when each side says, "There's only one way to do Army," and goes on to add, "and my way is the right way!"

Why not both?

If William Booth was anything, he was both autocratic and pragmatic. But that autocracy and pragmatism was clearly focused on his "bottom line." It was results that concerned him rather than the standardization of method. In fact, it was Booth's successors who were more involved in regularizing and policy setting. You can almost read the history in the statistical results. With the regularization of strategic methods and tightening up on creativity and flexible approaches to ministry came a dramatic slowing down of growth. But Booth could live with what others might see as chaos. You can imagine him counseling a new officer, "Do whatever it takes ... but win souls!" The greatest record holders hold the record for failures, too. Let's make more mistakes to win greater victories!

Ponder

One of the saddest things is that the fighting between generations of Salvationists as to who or what is right takes our attention off the "real thing."

This fighting is not limited to the generations, however. Even within generations people can be hypercritical. The USA Western territory discovered this when they planted New Life Centers in an effort to reach the Boomer and Buster generations of unchurched people. Were the New Life Centers successful in reaching those generations? Yes! Is reaching the lost what we are called to do? Yes! But the pioneer planters suffered tremendous stress from the criticism of other officers and soldiers who complained it wasn't Army!

I read a story recently that says it better than I possibly could. "Go down to the fish market and look into the crab barrel. They never have to put a lid on it because if one crab starts to crawl out, the others will grab on to him and pull him back down. That's what negative peer pressure does." Shame on us.

Probe

1. What symptoms of this situation do we see in our corps?
2. Why are things that way?
3. Is this good or bad?

Pursue

How can we improve the situation? Look for 10 ways and pick the best.

One generation will commend Your works to another; they will tell of Your mighty acts. (Psalms 145:4)

Preservationists vs. Traditionalists

I used to think that the Army was somewhat polarized, with traditionalists at one end of the spectrum and conservatives at the other. Now I have realized that much depends on how one defines "traditionalist."

If, by that term, one means someone who believes in keeping the spirit, spontaneity, pragmatism and flexibility of Booth and his early movement, then I believe that does define traditionalism. If, on the other hand, one defines a traditionalist as someone committed to keeping Booth's methods intact, then I believe a more accurate description would be "preservationist."

Booth was, before becoming a Missioner, a Methodist. Many Salvationists still are "methodists," locked into methods that were both contemporary and highly effective in Booth's day.

But here is a thought. If preservationists had been around millions of years ago, toting signs that read "Save The Dinosaur," we'd probably be able to look outside today and see dinosaurs walking around. Perhaps now we see dinosaurs of a different type because of preservationists!

Surely, the challenge for a real traditionalist is to look within Booth's methods and discover what principles he was striving to implement, then to take those same principles and explore how they might be dynamically applied to be as effective in our day as they were in his.

Are you up to that challenge?

Ponder

One of the challenges to older, "established" Salvationists comes when younger generations ask us why we do things the way we do. Often the end becomes the means and questions of "why?" make us feel uncomfortable because our only answer is to say, "we've always done it that way!"

Consider the story of the young married couple. The wife was cooking her first turkey dinner and she started by cutting off the legs of the turkey. "Why do you do that?" asked her husband. "Because my Mom taught me to," replied the wife. "Ask her why," urged her husband. She did, and Mom said, "Because Grandma taught me to."

"Let's ask Grandma why," urged the husband. They did, and Grandma said, "I cut the legs off because the turkey wouldn't fit into my little pan!"

Examine everything you do in your corps and ask, "Why?" If you have no answer, you may want to redirect your energy. As the trainer said to the jockey, "When the horse is dead, dismount!"

Probe

1. What symptoms of this situation do we see in our corps?
2. Why are things that way?
3. Is this good or bad?

Pursue

How can we improve the situation? Look for 10 ways and pick the best.

For God did not give us a spirit of timidity, but a spirit of power ... (2 Timothy 1:7)

A Pristine Army

If you had asked me a few years ago where the most pristine expression of The Salvation Army was in the whole world, I would have said the Army in the United Kingdom.

I would have said that primarily because of the number of corps that still have bands and songster brigades, and that hold open air meetings as well as two or three indoor meetings every Sunday.

In other words, I would have decided based on my image of what the Army has been for a major part of my life.

However, and this is no secret since the statistical record is there to be seen, one has to say that "it"—that pristine Army—is not working as well as it once did.

I heard of a Canadian who, when asked about banding in Canada, said, "It's the best and worst of times ... bands have never been better, but there have never been fewer of them!"

That, symptomatically, makes my point. It's no good being the best archer in the world if you are fighting an enemy equipped with laser weapon technology! We have to ask whether our commitment is to past, present or future generations. Proverbs says that "A good man provides an inheritance for his children's children ... " (13:22). Is our commitment to personal comfort levels or to mission effectiveness?

Or, to put it more simply; for whose benefit do we do what we do, ours or others? What was it Booth said? ... *Others!*

Ponder

Since we are talking of a pristine Army, let me share with you a thought that has been vexing me. Why do armies go to war? To make soldiers of the oppressed, or to free them? Our primary purpose, surely, is to free those who are captive to Satan. Our hope is that some of the freed will become soldiers so that the Army can continue to fulfill its purpose effectively. But, if conferring the rank of "soldier" and counting the increase becomes the priority we have a problem. If you have soldiers, but they refuse to fight, do you have an army? Soldiership implies that the holder of that rank is committed, hard–working, and willing to die to accomplish the aims and objectives of his army; what if those characteristics are truer of some non–soldiers than they are of soldiers? Is an army's power released by the rank, or by the actions of its people regardless of rank?

What if we only accepted those who were prepared to fight to get into such an army? Would it, like the reborn UK military, be a leaner, meaner fighting machine using modern weaponry?

Is the commitment in your corps to personal comfort levels or to mission effectiveness? Where should it be?

Probe

1. What symptoms of this situation do we see in our corps?
2. Why are things that way?
3. Is this good or bad?

Pursue

How can we improve the situation? Look for 10 ways and pick the best.

Wake up! Strengthen what remains and is about to die, for I have not found your deeds complete in the sight of My God. (Revelation 3:2)

The Challenge of the Crumbling Water Pipes

My wife and I once visited an ancient English city. While there, we listened to a television news report about a major problem the city was facing because its old water supply pipes were crumbling.

It took me back to the days when I was an environmental health officer in Chelsea. Even in those days the authorities were forever digging holes for various purposes. At one such site, they had uncovered some water supply pipes from Roman times that consisted of hollowed out tree trunks narrowed at one end in order to fit one into the other.

Since the pipes in this other city were described as crumbling, I imagine that they were not wooden but of some other construction.

The report went on to say that the city had, in fact, found a solution. They were busy threading new pipes through the old crumbling pipes so that, when the old ones finally disintegrated, there would be a brand new system in place.

It struck me that what was being described was a solution for every old church that, in its day, had been an effective conduit to carry the "water of life"—the living Word—to the unsaved. Churches cannot avoid the onset of obsolescence. That is, the "living water of life" itself does not become obsolete, but the channel used to transport it can, and does. The reality is that different generations do have different values, interests, likes, dislikes, and different technology!

Maybe we should consider "threading" fax machines, email, the Internet and other modern modes of communication through and/or around our "old pipes!"

What do you think?

Ponder

I am at that time in my life where the earthly container of my soul is starting to crumble. Not seriously, but enough that there are times when my body doesn't want to do everything the brain tells it to. In fact, truth to tell, it couldn't even if it wanted to.

I am at the stage where the "water of inspiration and creativity" still flows, but I am becoming increasingly aware that one day it may well start to trickle or be cut off suddenly.

I have, therefore, for years been going out of my way to mentor people. Not to clone them in my image, but to open up their minds so that the water of inspiration and creativity within them will be released, even after I am gone.

Crumbling old pipes have a limited life. That's a fact!

Probe

1. What symptoms of this situation do we see in our corps?
2. Why are things that way?
3. Is this good or bad?

Pursue

How can we improve the situation? Look for 10 ways and pick the best.

Your people will rebuild the ancient ruins and will raise up the age–old foundations; you will be called Repairer of Broken Walls, Restorer of Streets with Dwellings. (Isaiah 58:12)

What Is the Natural Evolution of a Seed?

Chaos is a part of life! Did you know that there are some consult–ants whose initial intervention technique is to create chaos in an organization? They deliberately ask awkward questions that force people to consider why they do things a certain way, whether there is a better way of doing them and even whether they should still be done at all!

I believe that this approach produces a win–win situation. If after such deep soul–searching we discover that we are using the best methods, we have reaffirmed why we do what we do. If we discover even more effective methods, that's something that would not have happened without such appraisal.

Chaos is, of course, part of the natural pattern of evolution. A fetus, a chrysalis and a seed all go through a period of chaos as they evolve. Yet is not the baby the same life as the fetus; the butterfly the same life as the chrysalis; the plant the same life as the seed? Maybe not the same appearance, but the same life nevertheless.

What if the Army is still only in the seed stage of its development? A seed we have grown to love and treasure and hope will never change, but a seed nonetheless. What if the Holy Spirit is starting to split that seed to allow the plant within to follow its natural cycle of reproduction? What if the plant looks nothing like the seed from which it emerges?

You know what? After their chaotic period, when that new life matures, the baby will have a fetus, the butterfly will produce a caterpillar that will then produce the chrysalis, the plant will produce a seed ... just like the ones they came from.

Since we are against abortion in the natural realm, can anyone tell me why we are for it in the spiritual realm?

Ponder

God's design is to build His nation through a simple plan—procreation. This is a plan in which all Christians are to respond to God's call to share their faith. God aches to prevent the destruction of the lost whom Satan blinds to the possibility of new life. They will be lost unless they are reborn as a result of having the gospel shared with them by compassionate followers committed to birthing new Christians. Followers must understand that preventing such new birth is tantamount to abortion in the physical world.

So, isn't it odd that we know it is wrong to prevent the birth of new Christians, yet we often try so hard to preserve the past, thus preventing change and the emergence of new "babies." Isn't the resistance of older corps to the birth of new expressions of salvationism rather like a mother trying to push her baby back into the womb? It may be possible for a time, but it will almost certainly result in the death of both mother and child!

Probe

1. What symptoms of this situation do we see in our corps?
2. Why are things that way?
3. Is this good or bad?

Pursue

How can we improve the situation? Look for 10 ways and pick the best.

Let us not become weary in doing good, for at the proper time we will reap a harvest if we do not give up. (Galatians 6:9)

Part Three

Eliminating Choice is Not an Option

People today value choices as never before. Try buying Easter eggs. Wal–mart now sells well over a hundred varieties. Try purchasing a cup of coffee ... decaf or regular? Latte or cappuccino? Mocha or Irish?... The challenge is that of pluralism. People want choices!

How Do You Eat Your Oreos?

My favorite American cookies are Oreos. In England I like chocolate digestive biscuits. Regardless of where I'm eating them, I eat cookies in a certain way for maximum enjoyment.

How do you eat your cookies? I often ask that question in seminars. Some say they just cram the whole thing into their mouths. Others dunk theirs in a cup of tea or milk. Others break them into pieces.

Me? I start nibbling at the top in straight lines across until I have half a biscuit left. Then I turn the semi–circle vertically and start nibbling in straight lines until I have a quadrant left ... which I pop in my mouth!

What would happen if I bought a cookie factory and decided I would only sell the cookies to people who promised to eat them the way I feel they should be eaten? What if I put a little diagram in each packet showing how to eat the cookie and insisted that every purchaser sign an agreement to eat them as prescribed?

Cookie sales would go down, of course. People like choices.

What would happen if all the churches of every denomination all over the world worshiped in exactly the same way? What if they all used the same music, same translation of the Bible, same liturgy, same length and same sequence? "Sales" would go down, of course. Fewer people would attend. People like choices.

What if The Salvation Army were to say there is only one way to run a salvation meeting: my way! The way I enjoy it!

"Sales" would go down, of course.

Ponder

I think it is safe to say that when the Army was young there was tremendous variety in the meetings. For a start, it was a number of years before the shape of music ensembles settled down into a common pattern of the brass band. Then, too, there seems to have been tremendous creativity with the writing of new songs, words and music.

It is probably safe to say that few corps are exactly alike. In fact, there are corps totally lacking live music. For that reason, it is hard to advertise nationally with generic material that we are a church. "Bait and switch" advertising (where you offer something not available in reality) lacks integrity. In fact, many corps lack a salvation meeting altogether. The Sunday afternoon praise meeting was the first to go, and we are not sure whether to pour praise into the holiness or salvation meeting. Today in many places we have a kind of hybrid mix of praise and holiness (a "praliness" meeting) or a mix of praise and salvation (a "pravation" meeting) that can alienate both proponents and opponents of the emerging worship form. And the new emerging worship is surely birthed by the Spirit since it has swept like a fire around the world and through all denominations.

Since God is the ultimate Creator who undoubtedly enjoys the variety of worship offered, what is all the fuss about?

Probe

1. What symptoms of this situation do we see in our corps?
2. Why are things that way?
3. Is this good or bad?

Pursue

How can we improve the situation? Look for 10 ways and pick the best.

"For I know the plans I have for you," declares the Lord, "plans to prosper you and not to harm you, plans to give you hope and a future." (Jeremiah 29:11)

What Kind of Tea Do You Want?

Once upon a time, you could just go into a supermarket and buy a packet of tea bags. Have you tried that lately? Do you want regular tea or herbal tea? Decaffeinated or caffeinated? Orange Spice or Lemon Lift? Raspberry Royale or Cranberry Apple? Constant Comment or Cinnamon Stick? Mint Medley or Earl Grey? Cozy Chamomile or Plantation Mint?

It seems that new brands appear every week. That's not surprising, especially when you see the kind of community change that is taking place in many parts of the world. Trying to satisfy the needs of people from the West Indies, the Pacific Rim, Australia, Europe and many other parts of the world, as well as those of immigrant origin now native to a country, is a mammoth undertaking.

When there were no choices available, the world was simpler and people were glad to accept whatever the manufacturer offered. It was a product–driven market with basically two choices: Take it or leave it.

All that has changed. Even cars from the manufacturing line are made to the specifications of individual purchasers.

There is no doubt that rather than becoming a melting pot (conforming to the host culture), communities are becoming more and more pluralistic. That trend, with its built–in expectations, affects everyone.

The implication? Those who fail to see that "one size no longer fits all" will have a problem surviving. The church is no exception. How valid is the expectation that one fixed program structure will appeal to all kinds of people?

Ponder

One of my favorite stories is about a traveling salesman who arrived at his usual hotel only to find it jam–packed with clergymen at a conference. "How did you feel?" asked a friend. "Like a lion in a den of Daniels," he said!

Have you ever found yourself in that kind of situation? I have, on a plane going to Argentina via Chile. I was the only non–Hispanic and the only language spoken was Spanish. It was the same at a stop–over. I learned a new sensitivity to minority cultures. Of course, it is not just people who speak a different language, or are a different color, or originate somewhere else who are culturally different. Generations can be culturally different, too. It's a pity that we can't see beyond the head to the heart!

Probe

1. What symptoms of this situation do we see in our corps?
2. Why are things that way?
3. Is this good or bad?

Pursue

How can we improve the situation? Look for 10 ways and pick the best.

Enlarge the place of your tent, stretch your tent curtains wide, do not hold back; lengthen your cords, strengthen your stakes. (Isaiah 54:2)

Which Hotels Do You Prefer?

One of the joys of reading a lot and attending many seminars is that you pick up some good stories. Unfortunately, it's not always easy to keep track of the source. However, I am reasonably certain that I heard the following from Leith Anderson and that it is a true story.

It seems that the CEO of the Quality Inn hotel chain was having his hair cut and asked the barber where he was going on vacation.

"Reno," responded the barber.

"Where are you going to stay?" asked the CEO.

"In cheap hotels all the way there, because my wife wants to stay in the best when we arrive," responded the barber.

The CEO realized that the barber would not stay at a Quality Inn at all for that vacation.

Quality Inns have now added three more hotel chains to their business: Clarion Inns (top of the line), Comfort Inns (slightly less expensive) and Sleep Inns (economy).

Nothing was changed at Quality Inns. Yet business potential (in terms of people staying) was increased by 300% by merely adding three chains.

Is that a parable or what? Booth saw in his day that the poor of London couldn't afford the price demanded by the "Quality Inn–church" of the day. He started a "Sleep Inn–Salvation Army!" Have we become a "Quality Inn–Army"? What would Booth do?

Ponder

I love that story. It is such a perfect picture of what is possible if only we could accept that there are many ways of "doing Army," ways that might be much more attractive to those we strive to reach.

Why not have chains of the Army equivalent to Clarion Inn corps, Comfort Inn corps and Sleep Inn corps as well as the chain of Quality Inns (traditional corps) we currently have? Look at the Roman Catholic Church and the variety of expressions and dress it has, yet there is never any doubt that it is Catholic. In fact, I wonder whether there are denominations in heaven. The bottom line, surely, is lost souls won and brought into God's kingdom.

In my territory (USA West) we have traditional corps, adult rehabilitation center corps, Salvation Army New Life Centers and a host of Cross Cultural corps. They are not all Quality Inn corps but they are all Army.

What is your corps like? Is the cost of attending too great for some? Is it time to consider planting a Sleep Inn corps (or congregation)?

Probe

1. What symptoms of this situation do we see in our corps?
2. Why are things that way?
3. Is this good or bad?

Pursue

How can we improve the situation? Look for 10 ways and pick the best.

Now to Him who is able to do immeasurably more than all we ask or imagine, according to His power that is at work within us ... (Ephesians 3:30)

Part Four

On Going Forth and Multiplying

Living things grow by multiplication, and giving birth is the natural process of procreation. Should the "Bride of Christ" be a mother, too? Is birth control in the spiritual realm a wise policy?

What Is the Fruit of a Vine?

When I ask this question in seminars, the usual response (with a little coaxing) is "a grape."

"Good," I say, "Now what is inside the grape?"

"Seeds," comes the reply.

"So what will happen if we plant the grape seed in the right soil, at optimum temperature, with the right amount of moisture and some tender loving care?"

"We'll get a vine!"

"Great!" I say. "So, again, what is the fruit of a vine?"

"A vine" comes the answer.

"So what is the fruit of a Christian?"

"A Christian!"

"And what is the fruit of a local officer?"

"Another local officer!"

"An officer?"

"Another officer"

"A Home League?" (Answers start to slow...)

"Another Home League!"

"A Sunday school?"

"Another Sunday school!"

"A corps?"

"Another corps!"

John 15 talks of bearing abundant fruit, fruit that remains. The parable of the talents tells of rewarding stewards who doubled the Master's money. When Jesus told the disciples to cast out into deep water on the other side of the boat, they caught two (plus) boatloads! Multiplication seems to be the key to abundant fruit!

Ponder

Of course, there are sour grapes and seedless grapes as well as the variety with seeds. Maybe you have some of these varieties in your corps.

Both "sour grape" Christians and "seedless Christians" can actually hinder the spread of the gospel. Corps' "sour grapes" have the ability to gather other sour grapes around them and make vinegar. The "seedless grapes" tend to cluster together, too (sometimes as a whole congregation!). Both may be threatened by the notion of actually producing another fruit–bearing vine.

How many Christians have the people in your corps reproduced? How many local officers? How many officers? How many sections have reproduced themselves? How many new congregations, outposts or corps have you spawned? Are you into the abundance of multiplication, or are you still just adding? Maybe even subtracting?

Probe

1. What symptoms of this situation do we see in our corps?
2. Why are things that way?
3. Is this good or bad?

Pursue

How can we improve the situation? Look for 10 ways and pick the best.

I am the vine; you are the branches. If a man remains in Me and I in him, he will bear much fruit; apart from Me you can do nothing. (John 15:5)

How Much Do You Love Your Husband?

At the time of this writing, my wife and I have been married for 41 years. I remember the courting days well: time had no meaning. I walked on air, there were late bedtimes, butterflies in the stomach, etc. It's different now. I'm not saying I don't love her as much. I love her even more. But it's a different kind of love.

I am keenly aware of the value of time. I'm heavier than I should be, I'm not as light on my feet, I need my sleep so I go to bed earlier, and those butterflies don't tickle quite as much.

The church (including the Army) is described in Scripture as the "Bride of Christ." That implies some very specific roles and responsibilities. For instance, a bride should love her husband more than anything else. She should be supportive of his goals and life–purpose. She should be loyal at all times, defending him from criticism. She should share his joys and sorrows. She should be faithful to him at all times, and listen to what he wants and do it. She should keep the temple of her body healthy, and keep vows made to him. She should bear him children.

Is the Bridegroom happy with his Bride?

Ponder

Have you ever noticed that new people fall in love with the Army, often at first sight? I've met a number who have discovered us by accident and asked, "Where have you been all my life?"

Yet there are those within our ranks who look with disdain at these new people who are thrilled by what they have discovered. You can almost hear those "sour grapes" thinking, "What's the matter with them? When they find out what we are really like, they won't be so exuberant!"

The problem is that many of us have never had the joy of discovering the Army for the first time. We were carried in as babes, dragged in as toddlers, or pushed in as teenagers.

We should, of course, be asking, "What do they see in us that we don't see for ourselves?" If we discovered the answer to that question, maybe we'd fall in love with the Army—perhaps for the first time. Who knows what might happen then!

Probe

1. What symptoms of this situation do we see in our corps?
2. Why are things that way?
3. Is this good or bad?

Pursue

How can we improve the situation? Look for 10 ways and pick the best.

And we know that in all things God works for the good of those who love Him, who have been called according to His purpose. (Romans 8:28)

Where Does the Fruit Form on the Tree?

An apple doesn't look anything like the trunk or branches of an apple tree, yet within the apple are the seeds from which another apple tree can grow. If apple trees failed to produce apples, sooner or later, they would die out, because God has only provided one protective container for apple seeds: apples.

Now, I'm no gardener, and it is possible that what I have already suggested is incorrect, but I am talking about the way God set up His garden, not the way others may be striving to interfere with His creative plan.

I have never seen an apple actually growing on a trunk. They seem to grow on the branches attached to the trunk. The trunk has its part to play in support and conveyance of sustenance to the growing apples.

I suppose you could graft new shoots onto an old trunk, but they will still require the support and nurture of the trunk if they are to bear fruit.

Are you still with me?

Use your imagination. What would happen if an apple tree trunk kept nipping off the apples, or refusing to support or nourish them, because they do not in their present form look anything like the trunk itself?

This is a trunk, I might add, that once had its genesis as a seed inside an apple just like the one it now strives to reject.

Do I need to say more? Is the message clear to those corps who choose to be barren rather than bear fruit? I hope so.

Ponder

Have you noticed how anything different from the norm is exiled by the majority: the runt of the litter, the black sheep of the flock, the injured, the lame?

Have you also noticed how the general attitude of any community is that the minority should conform to the culture of the majority? You see it with attitudes toward immigrants. You see it in the reaction of congregations to new Salvationists. They have to earn their right to have input or to participate fully, don't they? It is only fair!

I live in Los Angeles at present, and I am very interested to see whether when the Hispanic immigrant population becomes greater than 50% of the total city population we will still expect that the minority adopt the mores of the majority. Or will our biases surface in glorious technicolor?

A cocoon, of course, looks nothing like a butterfly. Thank God that they are not rejected by butterflies, or else the butterfly population would eventually die out.

Probe

1. What symptoms of this situation do we see in our corps?
2. Why are things that way?
3. Is this good or bad?

Pursue

How can we improve the situation? Look for 10 ways and pick the best.

Ah, Sovereign Lord, You have made the heavens and the earth by Your great power and outstretched arm. Nothing is too hard for You. (Jeremiah 32:17)

Have You Noticed Babies Look Like Each Other?

It's true! Babies look far more like each other than they look like their parents. They may look like a parent when he or she was a baby, they may look like one when they grow to be as old. But, as babies they look more like other babies.

Think about it: babies are all more or less bald, they have no teeth, they make a lot of noise, and leak at both ends and are therefore decidedly anti–social.

Yet, as one travels around, it is probable that you'll hear something like this: "Well it may be growing, but it's not really Baptist, is it?" "It may be reaching a lot of people, but it's not really Presbyterian, is it?" "It may be an exciting place to be, but it's not really Anglican, is it?" "So, it is making a lot of soldiers, but it's not really Army, is it?"

They are talking about their new church "babies," their new plants, and the reality is that they *do* look more like each other at that stage than they look like the denominational "parent." But, I'll tell you this: The new Salvation Army corps of today looks and acts more like Booth's "babies" than what Booth's babies grew up to become. They exhibit that same spontaneity, playfulness, curiosity and daring that Booth's early Army possessed.

An interesting thing is that if we love the "baby" unconditionally, he grows up to be, in many ways, just like Mom or Dad. Doubt me? Look at today's Army. Don't some corps look more like their Methodist parent than they did as babies?

Every generation needs to have babies. It is not so easy when you are over a hundred years old! But it's not impossible.

Ponder

Can you see it in your minds eye? Some time in the future we will look around our territory and see corps at all stages of maturity.

Look, over there—a baby corps! Its Mom hardly seems old enough to have a baby, but see how she is caring for it, nourishing it, changing diapers and bathing it gently.

And, look over there—a toddler corps, and a young adult corps. There's a middle aged corps, and a little further over there—a senior citizen corps.

And ... look at that. A centenarian corps has just been promoted to glory! God bless it and the children it bore, and the grandchildren, too. All of whom will continue to have babies until they can no longer bear them ... then nurture the babies of their own offspring.

Can you see it? *Can you see it?* Or do you think all corps should act the age you think they should be?

Probe

1. What symptoms of this situation do we see in our corps?
2. Why are things that way?
3. Is this good or bad?

Pursue

How can we improve the situation? Look for 10 ways and pick the best.

Commit your way to the Lord; trust in Him and He will do this ... (Psalms 37:5)

Part Five

Keeping All Eyes on the Ball

Without a clear destination, it's difficult to plan the journey and steer the boat. Someone has said, "If you fail to plan, you plan to fail." There is a great deal of truth in that phrase.

Parable of the Hungry Horses

Imagine that two horses are tied together by their tails, one facing east and the other west. Each sees grass just a few feet from where it is standing. Both are hungry but neither knows that the other is as well. So they keep pulling against one another, each striving for the grass that is within sight but out of reach. As they pull, they get more hungry, more frustrated and more sore!

If they would only stop and evaluate the situation together, the solution would become obvious. They would agree to walk over together to one patch of grass and eat it and then walk over together to the other patch of grass and eat that, too. They will have agreed on a common purpose and pursued it together.

Those two horses may represent the struggles of a typical corps. Imagine that each section of a corps is represented by a horse. Imagine all those horses tied together by their tails (part of the same corps) yet each as it pursues its own agenda pulls against the others, creating a lot of friction and dust with little movement and a great deal of frustration!

The result is lots of busy work but, perhaps, not too much kingdom fruit being produced. If only they would stop and evaluate the situation together, the solution would become obvious.

Agree first on a common purpose. Then agree on what a picture of that purpose fulfilled would look like. Then pursue it ... together!

Ponder

This is not just a problem for smaller corps, nor is it a problem unique to The Salvation Army! I recently viewed a videotape produced by the Willow Creek Association in which Bill Hybels talks about the lack of alignment in his church, a church which several thousands of people attend and one which is considered to be a model church in reaching the unchurched Boomer generation.

Apparently, each of the programs in the church was pursuing its own agenda with little effort to bring all those initiatives together in pursuit of a homogeneous, all–encompassing vision. That parallels the metaphor of the horses. Hybels now is working with each program/ministry to encourage alignment with the overall vision and to maximize efforts in its pursuit.

It is easy for this to happen in Army corps as well. Leaders pursue their own vision with little appreciation for other programs and the overall benefits of working closely together. A good question for each corps section to ask is, "How is what we are doing aligned with our mission statement and helping the corps to achieve its overall vision?"

Probe

1. What symptoms of this situation do we see in our corps?
2. Why are things that way?
3. Is this good or bad?

Pursue

How can we improve the situation? Look for 10 ways and pick the best.

This is what the Lord says—your Redeemer, the Holy One of Israel: "I am the Lord your God, who teaches you what is best for you, who directs you in the way you should go." (Isaiah 48:17)

What You See Is What You Get!

When I was a kid, I was urged and finally convinced by my Grandpa to learn to play a brass instrument, though I had resisted it for years. When I finally did get started, I discovered both an interest and a natural aptitude for the cornet.

To further encourage me, one Christmas my father bought me a number of recordings of cornet soloists. It was in the days of the old 78 rpm records when you had to change the magnetic steel needle for each play. I used to play the records and then play along with them, not realizing that printed music was available. I had caught a vision!

I had no solo coach and so I was totally unaware of what was difficult and what was not. All I knew was that if they did it, it could be done. In other words, I saw good playing as the norm, not the exception. Whatever they did, I did, even though it took a little time to figure out how. The how–to may not have been right. For instance, I found I could reach a high D by playing a high C and standing on tip–toe! It could also be done by playing a high C and opening the water key! The point was that I caught a vision, and with or without skilled help that was the destination I made for.

It's the same for churches. Sure, church growth skills can possibly help you avoid obvious time–wasters. But once you grasp the vision you'll get there no matter what.

What if healthy, growing corps were the norm, not stagnant, moribund ones?

Ponder

Have you ever heard it said that Army corps were destined to be small? I have, many times. Do you believe that? History suggest there were some very large meetings in our early days.

Whether Salvation Army corps should be large or small is a subjective matter. We can say that without a minimum critical mass, self–support is more difficult. We can also say that it is difficult for visitors to remain anonymous in a small congregation. Worship, as it is depicted in Revelation, is a large celebratory event. And if worship on earth is supposed to be a foretaste of heaven, what should we expect?

What we *can* say is that we need enough "barns" to store the harvest, whether they be masses of small corps, or fewer but larger corps. Our vision must never be limited by the size of our present corps building, and a full sanctuary is not necessarily indicative of a healthy congregation. Whatever size congregation you prefer is fine, but be sure you keep planting until all the harvest is in.

What you see is what you get. What do you see?

Probe

1. What symptoms of this situation do we see in our corps?
2. Why are things that way?
3. Is this good or bad?

Pursue

How can we improve the situation? Look for 10 ways and pick the best.

Call to Me and I will answer you and tell you great and unsearchable things you do not know. (Jeremiah 33:3)

The Power of a Common Purpose

This concept builds a little further on the "Parable of the Hungry Horses" (pg. 62). If the various sections of a corps are pursuing goals that focus on different destinations, the reality is that the nearer they get to those goals, the further they tend to move away from each other. However, the reverse is just as true.

If all the sections of a corps were to agree on a common destination, they would immediately start to move in the same direction. That is not to say that they will all be doing the same thing. The kind of language you will hear, though, is, "How can we help the corps to reach its chosen destination? What can we do with our strengths and resources to make that journey easier?" Each section retains its individuality, pursuing sub–visions that arise out of the corps master vision.

Do you see what else happens? As each section moves toward the same destination, they get closer to one another.

Commonly accepted visions are a way to resolve conflict in corps since petty issues fade in pursuit of a greater cause. But beware of accomplishing what you set out to do without having another challenge before you. Celebrate the victories, yes! But move beyond them to even greater challenges.

The battle is not over until all the lost are won ... or Christ returns. Whichever comes first!

Ponder

I love the story told by Stephen R. Covey in his book *The Seven Habits of Highly Effective People*. He speaks of a visit to a hotel where the service was exemplary, with employees going out of their way to be helpful.

When he asked the hotel manager why, he was told that the hotel chain's mission statement was the key. Pursuing that,

Covey indicated that many companies have mission statements yet did not provide as good service. The manager asked whether Covey would like to see the mission statement for that particular hotel, one in harmony with that of the chain but pertaining to the local situation, environment and time. Everyone employed in the hotel had participated in shaping it. "Do you want to see the mission statement written by the people who greeted you last night?" asked the manager. Every department had its own mission statement cascading from that of the hotel itself, which in turn had cascaded from that of the hotel chain.

The concept is the same for visions. Agreeing on a common vision for your corps is like an orchestra; everyone plays from the same score as it were, even though each plays a different instrument. Makes sense, doesn't it?

Probe

1. What symptoms of this situation do we see in our corps?
2. Why are things that way?
3. Is this good or bad?

Pursue

How can we improve the situation? Look for 10 ways and pick the best.

Whatever your hand finds to do, do it with all your might, for in the grave, where you are going, there is neither working nor planning nor knowledge nor wisdom. (Ecclesiastes 9:10)

How Many Squares Do You See?

Look very carefully at the box below. How many squares do you see? It doesn't matter where or when the question is asked, responses always vary.

Some say sixteen; another will say "No! there's another big one around the outside." Then people look a little closer and someone will say "No! there are also four larger squares, each containing four smaller squares." Someone else might say "No! there is another square of four squares in the middle."

After a brief silence, someone offers "But there are also four squares made up of nine smaller squares ..." And yet another will say, "Ah! but don't forget that every square has an inside and an outside to its frame as well, so that doubles the number seen so far."

We've even had people who say "Look! if you hold the page up to the light and view the diagram from the other side of the sheet, that makes twice as many squares."

And so the banter continues until I say, "I didn't ask how many squares there are, I asked how many you see."

The point is that different people see different things, even when confronted with the same situation. There are corps about which people have said for years, "You'll never be able to do anything there," only to find that an officer will come in, challenge that assumption, and turn the whole situation around.

What do you see? God's vision is perfect ... 20/20. Try seeing your community through His eyes!

Ponder

A company sent a salesman to a third world country to sell shoes. He emailed his head office, "The prospects are hopeless here, no one even wears shoes." The company sent out another salesman. He was hardly there any time at all when he emailed the head office with the message, "There is an incredible opportunity for growth here—absolutely no one wears shoes!"

It is all in the seeing, isn't it? Not the looking—the seeing. Not the perception—the reality.

How many commissioning meetings have you attended where a new lieutenant is appointed to a place that everyone knows cannot possibly grow? He is, no doubt, counseled by some well–meaning but misguided officer to accept the appointment and serve his time, knowing that in a couple of years he will be moved. Can't you see Satan, rubbing his hands with glee about that situation?

Then you'll see someone appointed who enables that same corps to take–off. What happened? He saw more squares than his predecessors. What do you see in your present setting?

Probe

1. What symptoms of this situation do we see in our corps?
2. Why are things that way?
3. Is this good or bad?

Pursue

How can we improve the situation? Look for 10 ways and pick the best.

This is the confidence we have in approaching God: that if we ask anything according to His will, He hears us. (1 John 5:14)

Aiming for a Bull's–eye, or Firing at Random?

Did you ever hear the story of the cowboy who rode into the little Western town? On his way in he passed a barn on which there were a number of targets with arrows right in the center of each one. The only person around was a feeble–minded lad holding a bow with a quiver of arrows on his back.

"Fancy shooting!" said the cowboy. "Who did that?"

"I did!" said the lad.

"How on earth did you manage it?" asked the cowboy.

"Simple," said the lad. "I fired the arrows into the side of the barn, then drew circles around them!"

Isn't that often what we are tempted to do? We fire evangelistic arrows at random and then claim each to have hit the bull's–eye. We are busy, busy, busy—too busy to assess the effectiveness of what we are doing in terms of kingdom fruit. Are we more concerned with measuring degrees of activity and attendance than with counting souls won to the kingdom and being discipled into fully devoted followers of Jesus Christ?

It's easier, but kind of backwards, don't you think? Shouldn't we first put up the target and then shoot the arrows at that target, honing our skills until we hit it more often? Failure to hit the target is, surely, not the fault of the target, but rather a lack of skill on the part of the archer. Skills can be improved. If they help us hit the right target more accurately, shouldn't they be improved?

Ponder

"It is a leader's responsibility to, once in a while, climb the tallest tree in the jungle and look around in all directions to make sure work is progressing in the right direction" (another gem from Stephen R. Covey).

But when that leader realizes that some corrections in course need to be made and shouts down "wrong direction!" more often than not the workers yell back, "Don't bother us! We are making excellent progress."

Doesn't that say it all? We can be so busy doing what we love and counting activity and attendance statistics that we fail (or do not want) to examine whether any real fruit is produced. How stubbornly we can resist any attempts to encourage us to change direction because the cost in terms of disruption of our comfortable routine may be untenable!

It is so easy to build our vision around the notion of what we would like to see happening in our corps. A better question might be "Is what we want to see what God wants us to see, and does it reflect what we need to be to accomplish the assignment God has given us?" Now, there's a target to focus your vision!

Probe

1. What symptoms of this situation do we see in our corps?
2. Why are things that way?
3. Is this good or bad?

Pursue

How can we improve the situation? Look for 10 ways and pick the best.

When you make a vow to God, do not delay in fulfilling it. He has no pleasure in fools. Fulfill your vow. (Ecclesiastes 5:4)

How Tight Is Your Target?

Who are you trying to reach? I often ask that question and frequently the response is "everyone." I follow it up with the question, "How are you going to do that?" There is usually no response.

One thing we can say with certainty is that no *one* church can serve the needs of all people. Oh, certainly larger churches can offer more programs, but the reality is that our effectiveness is limited by the needs we can meet. And our problem, primarily, is not enough leaders.

So, if we can't reach all, who shall we concentrate on? This is not a new concept for the Army; Booth's primary target group was the poor of London.

Think about it. Is your goal to reach unsaved, unchurched people or to win back those who claim to be Christian but who no longer attend church? The strategy for each will be different.

Do you strive to reach children with parents who like McDon–alds, or parents with children who like Wendys? The strategy for each will be different!

Are you hoping to appeal to Baby Boomers, or Busters, or the Truman Generation (born during or before WWII). Again, each will require a different approach.

What you really need is to get a toe–hold somewhere in people's networks of relationships. It doesn't matter where, since as people invite their friends, relatives, acquaintances and others, all ultimately will be won.

But where do you start? You start among those whose needs you can best meet right now, remembering it's a beginning, not an end!

Ponder

The notion of focusing, at least initially, on a primary target group is not a strange one. William Booth's heart for the poor coupled with a vision of what Christ could do with that group led him to his destiny. He may later have had a grander vision of the world for God but only after he had gained a significant toe–hold in that local, poor segment of the UK population.

Even the four Gospels support the same concept. Why don't we have just one gospel embracing all of the historical record? Because, among other things, each targeted a different segment of society in ways to which they could culturally respond.

Think about it. What are the odds of reaching an aged, non–English speaking immigrant living below the poverty level, a wealthy retired snow–bird from Canada and a Generation–X skateboarder in the same gathering? Pretty remote, wouldn't you say?

So, who can your congregation best reach? Exclude no one, but pick a priority target group of the lost. Put your focus there and see what happens!

Probe

1. What symptoms of this situation do we see in our corps?
2. Why are things that way?
3. Is this good or bad?

Pursue

How can we improve the situation? Look for 10 ways and pick the best.

Let your eyes look straight ahead, fix your gaze directly before you. (Proverbs 4:25)

Part Six

Clearing Log Jams

Here I bring together some bits and pieces that may be helpful. I look at three ways to develop creative solutions to challenges, handling people resistant to change and receive hope from the most unlikely source ... Charles Dickens!

Peel Off the Onion Skin

One of the most frustrating experiences is to spend a great deal of time solving a problem, only to find when you have finished that you have been dealing with a symptom, rather than the cause of the problem. Consultants may differ in the terminology used, but many, if not most, will acknowledge that there is usually a key issue that causes many subsidiary problems.

I have, for example, heard the word "jugular" used to describe the main cause of a problem. One of my Fuller Institute mentors, Dan Reeves, uses this word and suggests that as a consultant pores over the data—studying it, praying about it—the "jugular" issue inevitably surfaces.

Personally, I like the analogy of the log in the stream. We have all seen it; a fallen log in a stream not only restricts the flow of water, but also gathers behind it a great deal of debris. Clear the log and all the debris rushes downstream. But spend your time on the little twigs that form the debris and you'll never solve the problem.

How to identify the log is the initial challenge. I find it helpful to gather a list of the symptoms people identify (See "Two Questions" pg. 2—these usually bring the "symptom debris" to the surface) and consolidate them. Then work backwards, asking of each symptom, "Why is this so? What is causing this to occur?"

Repeat this process for each new set of answers. By the time you go back five levels of "Why?" and "What?" the log(s) will start to surface. But, be cautious, solving problems only restores the "stagnant quo!" You can restore an antique chair until it looks like new. It will still be an antique. But, once, it was a contemporary piece of furniture!

Try a "Dos" and "Don'ts" List

Many job seekers have no idea what kind of setting they would really love to work in. Yet, as I have suggested earlier, "what you see is what you get!"

If people don't know what they do like, one way of helping them is to find out what they don't like! For example, ask them specific questions: "Would you prefer to work out of doors?" "No! I'd rather work indoors."

"Would you like to be in an office on your own?" "No! I like to have people around me."

"Would you like to work different shifts?" "No! I'd rather work regular hours."

"Would you like an office without windows?" "No! I'd hate an office without windows."

We can use this technique to help solve problems. If, for example, we want to ensure that visitors return but have no idea as to how to achieve this, try reversing the question. "How can we make absolutely certain that no visitor ever returns?"

Now make a list of your thoughts ... "Make sure the doors are locked when they arrive; tell them, if they do turn up, that they are not wanted; use in–house jargon whenever they are around to confuse them ..."

Go through your list one item at a time and next to each write down the opposite course of action: "Be sure the doors are open when visitors arrive; welcome them warmly; eliminate jargon when they are around ..."

How Do You Get a Tortoise to Run?

Getting my corps people involved in evangelism is like trying to get a tortoise to run!" Sound familiar?

Using an analogy to help develop creative solutions is another way of getting unstuck. Take the "needle in a haystack" analogy, for example. Forget about motivating the soldiery for mission for a minute or two and think about finding a needle in a haystack. How could you set about doing that?

For a start, you could sit all over the haystack until the needle attached itself to you. You might use a magnet ... the stronger the better! Then again, you could remove each piece of hay, carefully, until the needle was revealed. Consider how these solutions to finding the needle might apply to motivating the soldiery.

As I write, three ideas emerge: I could sit down with each soldier separately and explore why the notion of being involved in mission does not motivate him (perhaps he knows nothing of spiritual giftedness) ...

I could make involvement in mission so attractive that he couldn't resist ...

I could, methodically, remove each objection by stressing benefits that exceed the perceived cost.

Now, what about the tortoise? I could light a fire behind it ...

Dealing with Negative People

Do you ever wonder what St. Paul's "thorn in the flesh" was? Personally, I wouldn't be surprised if, since he was a change agent par excellence, it was negative people who are resistant to any change that takes them beyond their personal comfort level.

"Let's get back to the good old days of the Army!" How far back do you want to go?... Knee drills every morning? Three meetings? Two Sunday schools? Three open–air meetings every Sunday? Saturday open–air meetings?

Pursue those questions and you'll prove what I have suggested. People who want to go back only want to go as far back as their personal comfort level. The reality is, however, that even with the smallest change proposed (especially if it is not first suggested as a trial project) there will be those who want to start yesterday, those who never want to start it, and those who are prepared to stand back uninvolved to see what happens.

I used to think that the easiest way to deal with the situation was to identify those keen to proceed and move forward with them. Wrong!

Negative people can be like springs sticking tenaciously to their view. As you push forward with your allies, those springs compress until the pressure gets so great that they spring back with a force that can set you back further than where you began!

It is far better to share your newly formed plans with those currently opposed to change, respecting their views and asking them to identify problems they see. Write these down and ask them to suggest ways in which the problems may be overcome.

As they offer solutions, you gain ownership! Try it.

A Lesson from Scrooge

I wanted to leave you with a thought that offers hope and optimism, no matter what challenges you face.

It strikes me that there are some lessons to be learned from the life of Scrooge, the lonely old miser Charles Dickens wrote about in his novel, *A Christmas Carol.*

If you remember, it was just before Christmas and Scrooge had been particularly mean to his office clerk, the one with a crippled son, Tiny Tim. Scrooge was asleep, but restless, when The Ghost of Christmas Past visited him. The ghost took him to revisit events in his past life. Scrooge was forced to observe the poor choices he had made, the despicable way he had dealt with his fiancée and his business partner and the long–term effect that his actions had on his life and others.

His next midnight visitor was the Ghost of Christmas Future. This ghost took him and showed him the way his life would end if he didn't change his ways: in a pauper's grave!

But, finally, came the Ghost of Christmas Present who showed him the way life could be, if only he mended his ways. He did. He changed completely and began a brand new life, loved by all.

The graph on the next page tells the same story, graphically, and shows its application in a corps setting. The past shows decline. The line, projected as if no changes are made, hits the horizontal axis at a predictable point in the future. But, it doesn't have to be that way!

Changes can be made that revolutionize the future. It's a choice. Make the right one!

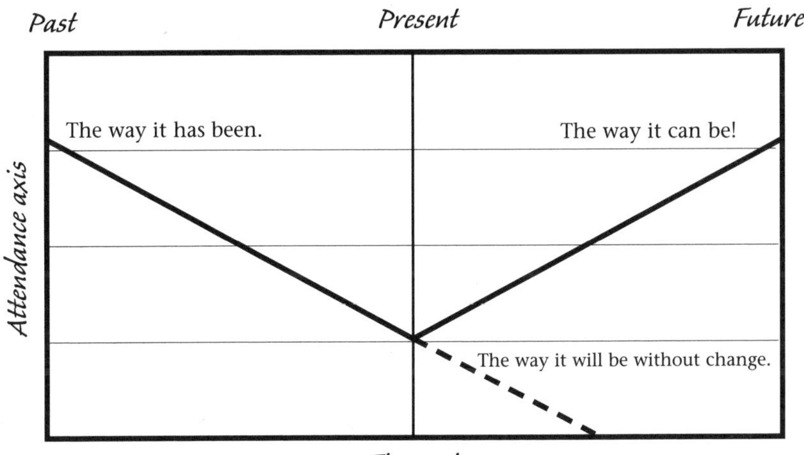
Past
Present
Future
The way it has been.
The way it can be!
Attendance axis
The way it will be without change.
Time axis